Come
and
See This, Folks

The biography of Jack Otter

Leicestershire's Naturalist

by

Anne Kind

with illustrations

by

John Stacey

V·O·L·C·A·N·O
PUBLISHING

Volcano Publishing,
13 Little Lunnon,
Dunton Bassett,
Leics. LE17 5JR

© Anne Kind 1994

Typeset in 11 pt. Times with headings in 14 pt. Garamond.

Printed and bound in England

ISBN 1 898884 01 3

In

Memory

of

Bill

Acknowledgements

To Loughborough Naturalists' Club
for permission to reproduce the illustrations
originally drawn by the late John Stacey.

David Ramsey

The *Leicester Mercury* for permission to reproduce
the photographs on pages 10 and 98.

Preface

For many years my husband, Bill, and I have been enthralled by the work of the well-known Leicestershire Naturalist, Jack Otter.

So many people have enjoyed either listening to Jack at his lectures or seeing nature in a different light on one of his many guided walks that it seemed to me that some sort of record should be made, not only for those who have met Jack but for others who would like to share in his enjoyment of the British countryside.

The first part of this book gives an insight into Jack the man, and extracts from lectures given at seven centres. The second part is an anthology of my own verse prompted by my experiences on Jack's residential courses.

My thanks for the help I have received go to:

Anne Sedman who audiotyped 36 tapes and assured me she enjoyed listening to them.

Bill, my husband, who taped Jack's lectures and stories over a 20 year period and who would have been delighted to know that they were being used in order to tell the story of a remarkable man, Jack Otter, who has helped so many people to learn about the environment.

Jean, Jack's wife, without whose constant care and encouragement Jack Otter might not have survived the trials and tribulations of the latter part of this century.

Contributions from Jean Cooper and others for their help in remembering some stories and anecdotes from Jack's courses.

Last of all my thanks go to Jack himself, who is a very

private man, for allowing me to interview him and for his help in making this tribute to him a reality.

First Residential Courses held here in 1971

Hallaton Hall
Hallaton, near Market Harborough, Leicestershire

Contents

Introduction .... (i)

Jack Otter 1

Come and See This, Folks

    Vaughan College 12

    Launde Abbey 16

    Horncastle 23

    Duncraig Castle 33

    Tan-y-Bwlch 39

    Flatford Mill 43

    Knuston Hall 45

    Malham Tarn 51

Painting Pictures with Words 55

List of Residential Course Venues 59

Postscript 60

Anthology of Verse

    Anne Kind 62

    Poems 65

Retirement 98

Books by Jack Otter 101

Jack's favourite tree – the Norway Acer

To Jack and Jean Otter

He and Jean are symbiotic
He needs her and she needs him.
She's the apple of his eye
Although the eyes grow dim.
She likes to cook for him and sew
Does tax returns and decorates
As well as lets him go.

The birds he loves fly quicker now
He's old and cannot see.
But he can stand and look at plants
And still embrace a tree.
He loves the life he's lived with Jean
Gives tribute where it's due
And if it hadn't been for Jean
"Nay folks, what would I do?"

A.K.

Introduction

It was on June 16th 1972 when we first met Jack.

I saw a yellow poster at Vaughan College Adult Education Centre, Leicester University; it drew my attention as a result of its colour. It was advertising a bird-watching weekend, to be held at the Convent at Hallaton – between Skeffington and East Norton in East Leicestershire – about 15 miles from Leicester,

I am a 'townie' and knew nothing about birds. Bill, on the other hand, had been taught bird-watching by his grandfather and had been a keen collector of eggs. The sort of things boys did as a matter of course in the twenties and thirties.

When I suggested that we should try the course, over a weekend, organised by Vaughan College, Bill readily agreed.

We had never heard of Jack Otter at that time. It soon became evident that the majority of people on the course were beginners with one or two experienced ornithologists among us.

Jack introduced himself, explained that his surname came from his Swedish ancestors (no, it was not a pseudonym) and that we could call him Jack, (most people were addressed by their surnames in those days).

Jack surprised and baffled us with his knowledge of Natural History. Not only did he give us facts of birds' behaviour, habitat and relationships to other species but he was able to imitate bird song. His free and easy manner and the way he delivered his lectures, were a new experience for us.

Jack could "charm the birds off the trees".

Introduction

We also discovered that although he would answer any question we put to him, the answers could be another lecture not scheduled.

After our evening meal in the beautiful panelled dining room, Jack took us for a short walk through the grounds.

We carried our binoculars, mostly rather new but there seemed to be nothing around for us to use them on.

All the birds were settling into the thick leaf cover for the night. Glancing over a gate someone spotted a very small rabbit sitting on a path, all alone. One by one binoculars were raised and adjusted to focus on the rabbit which stared at us with a bemused expression. Jack stood behind us and in a quiet voice we heard him say; "When he gets home his mother will say; nonsense, dear, you imagined it".

During that first evening, after our walk, we gathered together in the comfortable lounge, overlooking the garden and large trees.

The Hall is not a stately home. It is an early eighteenth century grey, stone house surrounded by a high, red brick wall. The interior consists of an oak staircase, panelled rooms and highly decorated ceilings. It was built for the Rev. Benjamin Bewicke, youngest son of Thomas Bewicke of Close House, Northumberland and Vicar of Barrow on Soar, in 1713.

It is now occupied by an Order of Nuns, called the Daughters of Our Lady of Good Counsel and St. Paul of the Cross, who

Introduction

purchased the Hall in 1951.

Listening to Jack telling us the programme for the next day I wondered what he could show us to make me interested in the wonders of nature.

We were mostly newcomers to birdwatching and I for one could not imagine how our tutor could help us to identify one bird from another.

I need not have worried. By the end of the first day Jack had captivated his audience and assured us that if we persevered we too would be able to identify birds and their song especially if we attended his classes at Vaughan College, we would soon master the art. He was not only a good teacher, he was also a good salesman.

He stunned us by imitating different birdsongs, pigeons' as well as stock doves, "but the one I can't do is the turtle dove", he would say.

"You will hear five times as many as you can see", he said.

"Birds are fairly easy. They move about on the wing. Flowers sit still for you to creep up on but mammals are difficult. They are the job for the patient dedicated person. You might have to rush around for bird spotting but with mammals you've got to soft-foot it. Go in ones and twos and never speak. Wear brown shirts and go out at dusk and dawn. You've got to be careful and you've got to study tracks and signs and pick up horrible little

Introduction

droppings. Mammals are different and difficult but they are rewarding and if you'll join my classes next winter, I'll prove it to you".

Jack paused for a moment and then continued; "Adult audiences who come to classes after a day's heavy work, want a different approach from the usual dry lecture.

Sometimes they have spent a day doing exacting work. They don't want to be sent to sleep. Retired people come to my lectures to enrich their retirement, they too want a different approach from the usual dry lecture. You can say one thing about the type of Natural History study we do in my classes....they're different".

To say that Jack had shaken us is an understatement. We were tired from walking all day but enraptured by our tutor's approach to the Science of Natural History.

It was agreed that Jack would take us to listen to the "Dawn Chorus" early on Saturday, around 3.30a.m. It did not appeal to me but Bill and a number of other stalwarts of the group met Jack, in pouring rain at the back of the Convent, in order to listen to the few birds prepared to sing in such awful conditions.

What Bill and I liked most of all about Jack was his sense of humour and his humility towards anything to do with natural history. "There isn't enough time to learn just a small amount of what I want to know", says Jack.

Introduction

This philosophy endeared him to Bill and a friendship grew from that first encounter until the day Bill died and beyond.

Jack made the birds he talked about become so real to us that we hung on every word he said. He told little stories in order to bring home certain points – a born teacher.

Jack Otter, Leicestershire's Naturalist

Jack was born in Leicester on June 14th 1909. "I belong to East Leicestershire", he would say explaining that his grandparents had farmed at Carlton Curlieu. His grandfather had taught him all about ecology although that word was not popular then. His influence has stayed with Jack all through his life and his love of birds and natural history stems from those early years.

Three people had influenced Jack in his youth; his grandfather, his mother and his father.

"There was no teacher who had more influence on me than those three people."

His grandfather had been a shepherd, was self-taught, a craftsman, almost an intellectual and a fountain of knowledge.

Jack's mother encouraged him in everything he was interested in. She gave him all he needed to make the things he wanted, a possibility. His father was a practical man. Jack recalls him doing up three bicycles and the three of them set off on outings into the countryside. Tilton-on-the-Hill and the Langtons were particular favourites.

They did not just visit beauty spots but sewage farms were on the itinerary in order to watch birdlife which could be found there in profusion.

Jack bred pigeons and canaries. His parents encouraged him in all his hobbies. Jack recalls his childhood at every opportunity. His grandfather, a shepherd and skilled farm-hand was a self-taught but highly observant field naturalist.

Jack Otter

"At an early age, he put me on the path to an extremely full and exciting life. I well remember over 70 years ago, how he pointed out to me in his lovely old cottage garden, the differing habits of thrush and blackbird. The one a hunter of snails, the other a stealer of grandfather's soft fruit.
We did not realise then but in fact I was learning the rudiments of ecology and the operations of food pyramids".

"In those far off days grandfather drew my attention to a phenomenon which I have occasionally seen since, the wonderful way in which a hillside covert had changed from blackthorn to mainly elder because of large flocks of roosting starlings. The general activities of the huge flocks had killed the blackthorn whilst elder seeds in the birds' droppings had germinated to give the covert a completely different character. For me this was a further big step towards a lifelong enthusiasm for, and, a growing understanding of the interaction of living organisms.

"When I was a boy of seven," he recalled, "I stayed with my grandparents at Carton Curlieu. Grandmother was the post-mistress and my mother and her sister – known as 'the girls', delivered letters in the area. One snowy winter's day, when I looked down the lime-tree avenue opposite the Hall I saw my first fox, a vixen with a cub. That first view of red against white has stayed with me ever since. On many occasions I've made students stop at a spot in a wood to ask whether they could smell that musty foxy smell".

That story about his mother and grandmother and how he saw his first sighting of a fox, makes us aware not only of the sights and sounds of the countryside, but also the smells.

Jack's enthusiasm for the natural world is what makes him such a good teacher.

"First things first" he would say "I'm interested in all plants, trees, animals, insects, and if the wife says, "have you posted that letter I gave you this morning?" I reply; "First things first".

"Long ago, when I was around 7 years of age I said to my mother; when I grow up I'm going to have an elephant.. Clean it, wash it, look after it.

I've got to over 80 years of age and I still haven't got one. Then one day I was asked to give a talk and afterwards they presented me with a large parcel. It was the picture of a large bull elephant".

Jack remembers an old double-fronted public house called 'The Fox' on the corner of Fox Lane where Lewis's Store once stood.
This was in the days when carriers' carts – each pulled by a strong horse – came in on Saturdays from Leicestershire villages. They called at many lonely farms where the carrier would collect orders and make deliveries during the incoming trip. They would then pick up orders from various shops and stores for delivery on the homeward journey.

Many villagers south and east of Leicester would wait and stand in the yard behind the 'Fox Hotel' so that customers might call with parcels.

Jack Otter

Jack's old aunt lived in a cottage at Illston on the Hill where he spent many delightful holidays "filled with birdsong and blossom".

"I often made that journey on the tailboard of that cart complete with my small carrier bag with my pyjamas and toffees. This was my holiday, an adventure in those far off simple times. We would leave Leicester on a Saturday and then return in a fortnight, sunburnt and full of memories".

He had many interests as a young man, among them was boxing and wrestling. He belonged to a boxing club in Humberstone, held in a big loft, as well as the Asfordby Boxing and Wrestling Club.

During the Summer the young men would go walking and swimming together. Club members would meet outside, wrestle and box on the grass, and after a cold shower consisting of buckets of water would towel down and then meet at the Windmill Inn, Humberstone, between Humberstone and Barkby Thorpe, for a drink.

When he left school Jack went to work in the shoe trade and then for Broughton & Jones, the high class ironmongers where he served the public and advised on mousetraps, grass seed and anything appertaining to what has now become a service of the past.

He remembers one customer who confided in him that she had a mouse which she wanted to get rid of.

Jack Otter

"I would like a trap for a mouse" she said, apparently thinking that 'nice' people did not have more than one mouse, certainly not mice.

"Now", explained Jack to his customer, "When you have caught your 'mouse', set the trap again and go on setting it for a fortnight. Mice will never lead a bachelor life for any longer than they can help", was his advice to a surprised customer.

At Broughton & Jones each year, seed was bought in bulk, and spread out in the basement for mixing and packaging. Jack's comment was; "The local mice sent out postcards to inform each other when the seeds arrived".

Jack's favourite seasons are Spring and Autumn, he loves Winter too but as for Summer, well, he and the sun never did mix well.

On wet days Jack used to be wryly amused by people coming into the shop complaining about the weather, especially if it was pouring with rain.
"The way some folks carry on", he would say, "You'd think it was liquid manure".

Many of his students – and there must be many hundreds who have attended his classes at Vaughan College and Crown Hills Community College, Leicester or at the Adult Education Centre in Northampton – joined him over weekends as well as weeks right across the British Isles. They will have walked with him in all weathers. My own recollections over the many years of our friendship, is that the weather was mostly fine.

5

Jack Otter

Now, whether that is my fantasy or a fact, I do not know, but it became quite a joke with many of us that even if it was raining 'cats and dogs' when we left Leicester, by the time we arrived at our destination for our Natural History Course, the weather would change and it would be dry and turn out fine.

On one such occasion Bill said to Jack; "Your hot-line to the Almighty has been cut, mate". The next day, when the sun shone, Bill was heard to remark; "Would you believe it, the line's been mended".

Jack used to talk about his wife to his students and would proudly tell them that Jean had made his jacket and his trousers and the waistcoat – far from impressing us it made us wonder who this paragon was.

The clothes looked perfectly tailored and it did not seem possible that they were homemade.

But it was so and when Bill and I met Jean, we were impressed by this delightful Scottish lass who could cook and look after her husband in order for him to do what he loved and did best, namely think and talk about animals and plant life.

Not only can she do all the practical things he has no inclination to do ("he isn't any good at...", Jean says), he was fortunate in finding a wife who could do his tax returns. I suppose it was a matter of self-preservation because Jack is no good with money. So Jean has to deal with everything. She even does all the decorating in the house.

Jack Otter

Jean told me that Jack went to see the Tax Inspector about some question of his earnings but the discussion got diverted and they started talking about birds. Jean asked him when he got home, "What about your tax?"

He replied; "Oh, that, I can't remember what he said".

"Right" said Jean, "I'll sort it out".

Jack and Jean met at a Labour Party Conference in 1953 in Margate. They found themselves in the same boarding house and as Jean said "We got on well".

Because they were the only two single people there, they were thrown together.

Jack had met Jean when they were both politically active. In Jack's case it was a superficial interest in as much as the connection that politics had on the environment. He was deeply concerned how the rape of the environment was going to affect us globally and how politicians only did whatever they could for their own good reasons – to keep themselves in their political niches.

Jack and Jean were married in 1954 and their only son was born two years later. Don, a much loved son, is his parents' joy and particularly as he has followed in Jack's footsteps by taking a great interest in everything his father said and did. His love of natural history is evident in his present position as warden of a large area of the National Trust.

"Jack was an excellent father"says Jean. "He took his corner right from the beginning". When Don was a boy, 2 years old, they went to Keyham, and back to Scraptoft – a round trip of

Jack Otter

four miles Jack explaining everything they saw and heard. It was history repeating itself, Jack having learnt all he knew from his grandfather.

Jean is the perfect match for Jack, she looks after him and he understands how lucky he is.

"Life's not fair", he once said to her, "I got you and you've only got me".

Jack is self-educated and when he began to teach adults at Vaughan College, Jean had to tell him how to pronounce the Latin names for different species.. It was Jean who edited the books he wrote, *The Birds of East Leicestershire* and *The Birds of Bradgate.*

He is always openly admiring and singing her praises. Jean said: "Jack always talked a lot, either on politics, the environment or philosophy.

His father called him the fighting parson.

He still likes talking to anyone who will listen," she says.

When I asked Jean whether he was easy to live with, her reply was, "Oh, yes, he is very tidy and methodical but he follows me about, always wants to know where I am. He sits in the kitchen while I am busy in there. When I go out he wants to know when I shall be back. When I'm a bit late he gets worried".

"You're late", he'll say.

"It's irksome, I could brain him sometimes. You see, I'm the original loner".

In 1977 Jack was invited to a Buckingham Palace Garden Party accompanied by Jean. While they were in the lovely gardens of the Palace Jack saw two beautifully coloured jays in the middle of London. He was quite excited at the sight.

Jean said to him; "You've come all this way to have a cup of tea with the Queen not to do bird watching".

In 1977 Jack was given an Honorary Degree of Master of Science by Leicester University for the work he had done for Adult Education in the City and County. A well deserved honour.

Bill and I were present at the ceremony at the De Montfort Hall and were very moved by the occasion.

A Celebration

Jack with his wife Jean,
celebrating his 80th Birthday at a party
held at Vaughan College in June 1989

(photograph Leicester Mercury)

Come
and
See This Folks!

Reminisences
of courses held at
some residential centres

Vaughan College
Adult Education Department, University of Leicester.

Each year during the first two weeks in July known locally as 'July fortnight' courses of varying interests are available for people who are not away on holiday. Jack's course is one of these and very popular it is too. The Natural History week of walks across different locations such as the Green Lanes of Leicestershire or Woodlands in the County and adjoining counties is enjoyed by many people.

The mornings are spent listening to the tutors and then a coach takes the students to their destination and brings them back to the College in the late afternoon. By the time we finish the course on a Friday afternoon, we are reasonably fit. We have probably walked several miles every day and seen and heard much of what is going on in the countryside.

First week in July 1990
Morkery Wood, Clipsham Wood, Wakerley Forest, Dalby Wood and Merrible Wood,

We hardly manage to clamber from the coach before Jack calls us, "Gather round folks, this is worth seeing".
It would have been surprising if it hadn't been, some of us think.
"Look at these king cups, mayblobs we call them, this is the build-up of a flower, the corolla, calyx, perianth, nodes, internodes, petiole, peduncle, filament...

...Daisies are composites, some flowers turn into seeds carried by parachute".

THE PARTS OF A FLOWER

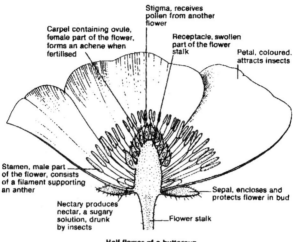

Stigma, receives pollen from another flower

Carpel containing ovule, female part of the flower, forms an achene when fertilised

Receptacle, swollen part of the flower stalk

Petal, coloured, attracts insects

Stamen, male part of the flower, consists of a filament supporting an anther

Sepal, encloses and protects flower in bud

Nectary produces nectar, a sugary solution, drunk by insects

Flower stalk

Half flower of a buttercup

Jack is prepared to admit when he doesn't know something and is delighted if one of the students can help him out. After all he came to botany much later in life, his original interest being zoology and ornithology.

The next thing he comments on is the litter we see.
"It is a scourge on the surface of the earth. You find a beauty-spot and if it gets known, people, cars and ice-cream vans move in. "Gonks", he calls them "they go to these honey-pots where there are lavatories and shops. These people are attached to their cars by an invisible umbilical cord. Still, nature has tricks to balance and control. Nature says – if you take what you want, you'll pay for it!

Vaughan College

As we approach the wood he draws our attention to the territory. "Listen to the sweet song of the blackcap singing just above us. He invariably sings on the edge of a wood. Look at the canopy and see the trees and the type of canopy. There goes the chiff chaff".

Very few birds can count!..but if anyone bent the edge of their nest the bird would know it and desert".

Then he continues to tell us about the bird we have just heard singing above us, the type of trees it prefers and; "Birds can't compare with humans, we haven't got a zip yet like the webbing of a bird's feathers".

Jack's comments are spontaneous and those of us who have known him for many years and have listened to his talks have heard them all before and yet we come back like children to hear their favourite stories again and again.

"Now then folks, come and look at this – hedge woundwort. It stinks you'll say. The least attractive member of the aromatic mint family, you think. But look at the beautiful silver markings on its purple-pink petals.

Enchanter's nightshade – each tiny flower like a miniature orchid: two petals, two sepals, two stamens, two pistils, like a bright new penny falling through the water of a deep pond".

Jack knows the local countryside so well that he can constantly surprise his classes. He can hear the approaching whistle of a kingfisher 100 yards away and knows its winding linear territory.

"Give me 15 seconds and we'll see a kingfisher" he'll say and the kingfisher whirrs round the bend on time.

"How do you do it, Jack?" we ask.

"I send postcards to the right places", he replies with a twinkle.

Launde Abbey, Leicestershire

Launde Abbey 1979

This weekend, proves to be a favourite with many of us who have become followers of Jack Otter.

Apart from the beauty of the house and surrounding country-side, it means we do not have to travel far. Approximately 15 miles from Leicester on the Oakham Road, Launde is tucked away in a valley surrounded by woodland. It is full of interesting flora and fauna and whenever Vaughan College advertises that Jack Otter would be running a weekend course there, it quickly fills up.

There is the usual welcome from the Warden who runs the place with his wife and after supper Jack talks about his plan for the weekend, where we are going on Saturday and what we are likely to see when we get there and what the weathermen have said about the prospect for the next few days. As for the past, well, there are so many stories he can tell, we only have to touch on a subject and he is giving us a lecture on it.

Wren

"This year the wren is the most numerous bird in Britain" he tells us; "according to the British Trust of Ornithology".

When we were on the Kyle of Loch Alsh, at 2,000 feet it was the only bird singing. 1963 was a bad winter, 8 weeks of solid deep freeze, killed a lot off. But they're back in numbers.

Launde Abbey

"I remember another year, snow up to my knees, dead grass underneath, I saw a wren going into a hole under the snow, feeding in the micro-climate below. I knelt down and the wren came out of another hole 30 yards away. He lives up to his name alright, Troglodyte – little cave dweller".

He continues; "Tomorrow morning. we are going to walk around the house and into the kitchen garden. We'll pass one of my favourite trees, the *Sequoiadendron Giganteum*. I find a great delight in Latin names although some are misnomers and awkward but some are delightful if you analyse them.

Sequoia was the name of an old Indian chief. The tree was named after him. He was a good man in his area and did well for his tribes. *Dendra* is a tree and *giganteum* is big so if you read it backwards, simply into English, it's the big tree of the Chief Sequoia. So never mind about the botanists' books, when you see it tomorrow morning. think to yourself, the Big Tree of the Chief Sequoia".

Jack continues to tell us the list of birds we are likely to see – sparrowhawks, tawny owls, their flight and how to recognise them and how the owl hunts. We might see a woodpecker and we would surely hear it. He talks about the animals we might see, deer, voles, wood-mouse or fox, stoat or weasel. Then comes a story of his early days as a schoolboy learning about Natural History from his grandfather.

Lesser Spotted Woodpecker

"Over 70 years ago, on a cold, grey morning in autumn, I walked through the old stackyard of the farm where my grand-

Launde Abbey

father worked in the village of Carlton Curlieu, South East Leicestershire. The broad passage between two rows of stacks was, as normal, littered with chaff and seed and at that moment being exploited by a large mixed flock of finches and sparrows. As I entered at one end a sparrowhawk came in at the other. She came in fast, yellow eyes glaring and flew just inches above ground. She took the flock by surprise and picked up a chaffinch. Then, with the prey in her talons, flew right past me and out by the way in which I had entered.

This was a perfect kill and such an exciting thrill for a young schoolboy that even after seven decades, the memory still forms a vivid picture".

He talks about Leicestershire being fox-hunting country. How he approves and how without the hunt there would be a shortage of woodlands and of woodland communities. Woodlands are managed by landowners who take part in fox-hunting so that it results and helps in conservation.

Jack has had many sightings of foxes in his life especially in the Launde area and he recalls one near Loddington which stood in a clearing in the middle of hundreds of bluebells and the beauty of it, of the red fox with black tips to the ears, the green bank and the bluebells. A sight not to be forgotten.

Then Jack whets our appetite by telling us of a badger's set which we would find nearby.
Badgers walk on their heels like bears and man. "These are the creatures who live here; *we* are the visitors!"

Launde Abbey

He brings natural history to life and makes us look forward to the next day's adventure. We never know what we are going to find.

After breakfast we all meet outside the house dressed in our walking boots and according to the weather, a variety of clothing suitable for a day spent in the open air. Jack is usually the first to be ready for our day's walk. He is dressed immaculately and his shoes are always highly polished. "You can see your face in them" says someone in our group.

The next day is spent as promised outside, walking through the wood or on the edge looking for interesting specimens. We hear wood-pigeons and Jack talks about them. He mentions the difference between them and collared doves. He first saw them when he was in India during the Second World War.

TheCollared Dove

"Their oesophagus is special. Their crop holds food and softens it. Thick milk or cream sloughs off the inside of the crop to feed baby birds for a few days. It is interesting to note how pigeons drink. They put their heads into water and suck. No other birds do this. They fill their crop with corn quickly in order to fly away as fast".

We climb up the grassy hill towards Big Wood and Jack is talking as we enter the wood. There it is, a patch of bright bluebells among the greenery. Jack knows every inch of this area.

A number of birds are singing and he stops us.

Launde Abbey

The Blackcap

"There over on the right is the sweet sound of the black cap, as well as a wren". I learnt that the blackcap sings high in the trees at the edge of a wood. Jack has told us this several times and, most of us being older, we don't always remember what we are told! Frequent repetition helps.

In the distance, a cuckoo is calling. "Now, cuckoos, I'll tell you about them tonight", he says, "they come in the springtime and mate with anybody they can find, and shout 'cuckoo' and flounce about and have nothing to do at all. They have a wonderful time. The female watches and waits and finds nests and gets the eggs all fostered properly. She can hold up the laying of her eggs....Women do all the work!...geese take up to an hour to lay an egg but a cuckoo can lay one in one or two seconds. She nips in while the foster bird is away from the nest.. Most cuckoos in this area go away by August. Young cuckoos may be in the nest till September. They gather together in little bands and fly to the same place as the old ones. Amazing...cuckoos can live approximately 20 years. Yes, I'll tell you about them tonight".

The Cuckoo

Launde Abbey

Jack is walking and talking, all the time surrounded by his students and they in turn stop him when they find something of interest. Someone at the back of the line of followers will call... "Jack, come and look at this".

If Jack thinks it is of interest to the group he suggests that the specimen is kept until it can be discussed during the evening lecture. This can be anything from an unusual grass to a fox dropping.

Jack points out the trees, their shape and the canopy; "The outer branches of an ash tree all curve gracefully upwards like the antlers of a stag." Jack has a turn of phrase reminiscent of poetry.

He points out the four layers of the broadleaved woodland.
1. The layer we walk on.
2. The layer we walk through, herbs and plants from 12 inches to 2 to 3 feet high. Dogs mercury is a good example. It flowers before the leaves come on trees, then becomes a good shade plant.
3. The layer we duck under – shrub layer – elder, guelder etc.
4. Canopy layer, large trees, oaks etc. Pedunculate for timber.

The oak tree is the richest of all. It is a living ecosystem. A man could study an oak tree for the whole of his life. The oak has the greatest gall activity. There are 60 known species of gall. Provided the load is not too big, the tree will survive.
All the different layers in woods are important. Each layer supports all sorts of wild life, particularly insects. Insects outnumber all other animals 3 to 1".

Launde Abbey

The Spotted Flycatcher

On our way back to the Abbey we pass the pond and see a flycatcher, sitting alone on the branch of a tree overhanging the water.

We stand with binoculars raised, quietly watching it whirring upwards to catch an insect and then in circular flight getting back to its original position.

We find the skin of a grass snake which Jack then takes back for later discussion.

"They have a serpentine movement, no animal moves with such beautiful grace", says Jack.

"Now then folks, come and look at this....field maple, one of my favourite trees and a relative of the sycamore.

Stop your clacking folks and listen to that blackcap's song. Short, clear notes, nightingale-like clarity...our best warbler...how can people enjoy pop music? And there's nothing in the world like our springtime dawn chorus.

Some folk...if there's nothing on telly, they're licked. I've never been bored in my life.

I hear people at the back talking about where they went on holiday last year. I say, never mind where you went last year, you're in this wood Now!!!!

Look, feel, taste and never stop listening. It's a wonderful world and we must look after it for those who come after us. And whatever we do we must never let go of the JOY!!!

That's what it's all about.

> *"Two men looked out through the prison bars;*
> *One saw mud and the other saw stars".*

Horncastle, Lincolnshire

Here we are in Lincolnshire. It looks like a patchwork quilt, divided up by coloured fields of yellow, brown and green, and the bright blue sky above us.

We are staying in the Adult Education Centre in Horncastle and one of Jack's favourite places – the food is good.

The areas which Jack likes to show his students are visited on a yearly rotating basis.

This time it is Kirkby Moor – bought by the Lincolnshire Trust – Snipedales and Theddlethorpe dunes.

Jack tells us we are likely to find halophytes, (goosefoot family), buckthorn, and, marram grass – how it spreads and sends out runners.

He talks about the natterjack toad with a yellow line down its back and adders and lizards on Kirkby Moor.

"One year we saw 24 adders after a lot of rain and then sunshine. They all emerged to sun themselves. They are not dangerous really. As long as you leave them alone". He picks up snakes and knows how to handle them by holding them by the neck.

Snipedales is wonderful rolling country where we see skylarks but mainly hear them all day.

"Turn over debris, see what's underneath it. We are all beginners trying to learn, peep into everywhere and then introduce our finds to others. I always say the best questions always come from beginners".

During the evening lecture Jack shows us a badger's tail which someone has picked up within 6 yards of a set.

Treecreeper

We see a treecreeper during the day which decides Jack to draw a woodpecker on the blackboard, detailing the 10 special points about a woodpecker's body. The drumming sound is used in place of a song in the pied woodpecker. Treecreepers behave in a similar manner in the way they creep up trees like a woodpecker.

He is very good at drawing particularly on the blackboard. We are told about the nuthatch which does not use its tail but supports itself by its feet and climbs any way up or down or around trees.

"We're going to do the same thing tonight, which we always do, looking at things we've seen and just having a peep further in. You can peep in 50 or 100 ways like this with each subject. If you really go to town you can take any of the points we have raised and look into it for a week and keep digging up new things".

During the day several skulls are picked up, possibly rabbits' or hares'. They have two rows of incisors and no canine teeth. One of the members says; " My dog has teeth like that".

Jack replies; "That is a malformation",

"No", is the reply, "it's a terrier!"

Jack's sense of humour has spread to his students.

Horncastle

Someone points out robin's pincushion on a wild rose. This results in Jack explaining about galls. They are the effect of larvae and eggs on growth of tissues on plants. The effect is often quite beautiful. Robin's pincushion is a gall.

Robin's pincushion gall

"We should be able to recognise gall manifestations even if we don't know what it's called. Too heavy an infestation would be a bad thing for a plant but many plants can stand a certain weight like a dog can stand so many fleas. If he gets too many fleas it's going to pull him down. 'Gall' means to irritate. It is regarded as some form of irritation. It's 'galling' to the plant" he says amidst peals of laughter.

Oak marble gall

Horncastle

He tells us that one of his favourite plants is bog cotton which is found in profusion in Lincolnshire. It is a sedge with three-cornered stems. The real cotton plant is part of the mallow family.

Beautiful damsel

Golden-ringed dragonfly

One of our group calls Jack to look at a damselfly which hovers in front of us.

Jack says "There are 45 species of damselfly and dragonfly in Britain. They are fast flying savage predators. Dragonflies perch with wings outspread. Damselflies close their wings. Transition of their lives is lengthy and most interesting. The larval stage takes place under water and as the insect emerges from the pupa it is like 'a lady wriggling out of a girdle'. Then on its first flight it goes 20 yards down river, drops on to mud for a rest, a water hen comes and gobbles it up.

That's Nature for you".

We find lizards on Kirkby Moor, they are much quicker than snakes.

We come across a squirrel's drey but no squirrel. Still, that does not deter Jack from telling us that they are vermin but charming with it. They have big strong back legs and steely claws. When a squirrel jumps from tree to tree he jumps into mid-air, holds his muscular tail straight out, holds himself on course (does not actually steer) hits the tree with all feet then runs up and goes along branches like a ballet dancer.

Jack points out sphagnum moss; "It is absorbent to an almost unbelievable degree". It contains chemical means for drying without rotting. It is absorbent and sterile when dead. It was used during the Battle of Waterloo as a dressing for wounded soldiers. One of the group tells us that women in Scotland during the First World War were paid to collect moss for dressings. It was used during the Second World War to absorb pus from infected wounds. People had also become aware of its deodorant properties.

As we walk Jack is talking; "I love Lincolnshire, my great-grandfather farmed here, it's not just potato fields and pea fields, you can breathe here, it's home territory to me".

Reed Bunting

We spot reed bunting during the morning. "They are always exciting birds. I still get a thrill when I see them. I am very very sorry for anyone who loses that sort of thrill. They always have a small song-post like a little bush. The hen incubates in the grass somewhere and there he sits in his beautiful brown coat, grey waistcoat, a black cap and a white collar. He's a lovely little bird. When he's finished moulting he looks very much like the hen. Altogether a charming little bird, the locals call them 'fen' sparrows".

Horncastle

As usual one thing leads to another during the evening's lecture. It typifies Jack's deep interest in the environment and his enthusiasm is catching. One of the group had seen five turtle doves on the ground feeding, she tells the group that she had been dying to tell someone about it

"Yes", said Jack, "I know the feeling. When I was out in the Far East during the war, the first session was rigorous training in Ceylon, it was wonderful for me, all the wildlife out there, the elephants and leopards and the bird life, I identified over 250 birds. I used to be so excited but there was nobody to tell. 600 men in the regiment and all they thought about was bingo and the only man who was interested was the Colonel. Now and again we could get together and have a talk – normally you wouldn't approach a Colonel".

When he was asked how he identified the birds in the Far East without a book he replied; "I have always read about other countries, studied them and visited museums so that I know about the birds but did not know the different species. Not for the first 12 months though, so I had to learn patience."

Sandpiper

"I will tell you something I saw when I was in Ceylon. They were irrigating the canals. A pack of sandpipers were feeding on the mud. A kite tumbled in, and took a sandpiper. He fumbled his catch and dropped it. The sandpiper fell into the mud and rolled. The kite turned over in mid-air to come down and retrieve it, the sandpiper tried to struggle to its feet and I started to run forward to take it from under his nose but none of us had a chance. The expert was coming in over the jungle. The first thing I heard was the wings, as a peregrine falcon came in and she came in under the kite and picked up the sandpiper. It was a beautiful exhibition by the expert. Now you see the difference between hawks and falcons. Granted they are all birds of prey but there are three groups.

Falcons – peregrine, kestrel, hobby, merlin – all fast and muscular.

Hawks – buzzards and eagles, golden eagles, sparrowhawks, goshawks – ordinary killers with yellow eyes.

Fish hawks – osprey.

The kestrel can 'stand' 100 feet up and plummet down to grab his prey. The peregrine falcon, small, puts all eagles to shame. He is an expert killer. I have never seen this but I am told that she can stand over a duck flying beneath her and go into a power dive at 150 m.p.h. (this has been tested), come hissing down through the air and take the head off a duck in flight. Accuracy and courage are needed, as the force could break her own leg. Such accuracy and such delicacy. She throws the head away and comes back and retrieves the body".

"Yes, the falcons are the most exciting".

During the day Jack had mentioned lichens.
One of the group has a question unrelated to birds of prey.
"What are lichens, what are they exactly?".

Jack replies: "There are five living kingdoms, but mind you in 40 or 50 years they'll sort it out again. The experts are always changing their minds.

These are *monera* – single cell organisms without nuclei.

protista – single cell organisms with nuclei.

Plants.

Fungi – neither plants nor animal.

Animals.

Lichens – a fascinating partnership between plants and fungi.

Animals – amongst which we might find crab, starfish, sand-hoppers and springtails. These latter are often found in pools of water after a rainshower. They look like grey dust, jumping," Jack warns, "but if you look carefully you can see they are springtails so look for toads in little ponds, they are the natterjacks".

The natterjack toad breeds here and we would find saltwort, glasswort, sea-blights and sea purslane on the area washed twice a day by the tide. Sea buckthorn takes over many dunes and acts as a shelter for migratory birds. We would find marsh orchids and golden yellow irises.

Jack continues, "On the moor there are three kind of heather and if we are lucky we might find moonwort. Although it is difficult to find. You may also see and hear redpoll and shelduck and maybe we'll see some adders.

I love snakes" says Jack, "people have horrible prejudices about snakes, they are cool, dry and silky to the touch. The male is black and silver, the female black and gold. If you are afraid of animals, don't fiddle with them or handle them. One year we were lucky, we saw two dozen adders just after they had come out of hibernation. They disperse within twenty-four hours usually".

Snipedales is a Nature Reserve and is wonderful for primroses, water avens and conifer trees. "I'd sooner see a few conifer plantations than have bare mountain slopes where broadleafed trees won't grow".

Shelduck

Swallow

"One thing I want you to see and I'm sure it will be there again this year, and that is the swallow's nest. Each year the same nest is there. Under the iron grating over the water pump for the use of farms up on the hills. It may even be the same swallow each year. As we approach the nest we usually see her come through and out of the passage with beautiful control at 30 m.p.h. So, look out for the swallow's nest".

Now Jack turns to other aspects of Natural History.

"The most obvious background in an area is the parent rock. From parent rock and then to soil and then plants.

The next important aspect is the plant life. The most obvious background to any study are the plants in an area. The natural world is fascinating. Like painting the Forth Bridge, you never reach the stage where you can go out without your books. It is all so complex and beautiful".

This leads him to tell us about the Great Ouse river which had been diverted for many years so that it did not silt up Saltfleet Harbour.

Another line of dunes had formed behind and now there was marsh-land between the lines of dunes.

Gradually the talk and discussion ends in taking out maps and we are told where we are going to walk during the next day.

Jack says; "Well, folks, the plan for the weekend is to visit the following places; Theddlethorpe Dunes, Kirkby Moor and Snipedales".

Duncraig Castle, Wester Ross, Scotland

"This is the most wonderful area in Britain", Jack said at the assembly after our arrival.

We are in pine marten country. This mammal was once a common woodland beast but owing to persecution it is now only to be found in remote places like the Lake District or in Scotland. It resembles the stoat but is larger with longer legs.

"This is my kind of country. Once when I visited this part we identified 78 species of bird here and 26 of these were unusual and exciting ones. Some people don't realise the beauty which exists around them. I call them Gonks, they don't know the difference between a flower and a cow dropping.

We're going to see red throated divers, they're built like a submarine, streamlined, propelled from the back. They toboggan on their bellies into the water.

Thirty years ago when I was here with some friends we were sitting by the loch having a last look at the black throated diver and its family, a black cloud hovered above us and then there was a snowstorm. We had to wrap ourselves into anything we had got. One of my friends who was a botanist was most displeased. He wasn't excited about seeing the black throated diver.
"That's it," he shouted, "you said a week ago we'd take it easy for the first few days. Watching the black throated diver in a bloody storm...".

Those of us who have known our tutor for some time knew that this story was no exaggeration.

Duncraig Castle

He continues;
"This area has four species of grouse and if we're lucky, we'll see some of them". We do. At least three out of the four.

We saw a capercaillie – I thought it was a turkey – walking across the road. We also saw black grouse and ptarmigan.

We climb one of the many mountains around Plockton. Jack tells us to keep very quiet. Suddenly the rocks begin to move and we realise that we are in the midst of around 20-30 ptarmigan. The birds are indistinguishable from the rocks, they blend in perfectly. Nature's way of making sure that the species will survive.

Stonechat

We hear the sound of two stones being knocked together and are told that this is the stonechat, a delightful little bird, not unlike the whinchat, but preferring rougher country and stockier and more upright than the whinchat.

Some of the botanists among us find common figwort. Jack explains; "Mysterious looking little flowers with deep purple red hoods, like real bad blood from a big vein and little cream faces underneath the purple hood and a nice square stem, a real beauty, about three feet tall. Damp woods suit it best".

Some of us visit Loch Torridon and walk behind numerous sandpipers and watch them for some time and we could have stayed on for a long time if it had not been for the midges which are large and bite us mercilessly.

The Meadow Pipit

We thought we saw tree pipits today and Jack explains the different types and their flight. These little birds are common in open woods and clearings but the bird we saw and heard here in Scotland was the meadow pipit. Its call is a thin 'zeep'. The song usually given in song flight is weak, ending in a trill.

That evening after dinner a small group of us go for a walk. It is getting dark. On looking up at the tall pines surrounding the castle where we are staying, we see a long-eared owl looking down at us. What a magnificent bird. It is as silent as the night. We never saw another.

Jack who was not with us at the sighting was pleased for us. This gives him an opportunity to talk about owls.

Long-eared Owl

"Owls keep their feet on the branch on which they sit so quietly, looking down at anything which moves. When they mark a mouse they never move their feet because they make a noise and could frighten the mouse off. They keep their feet still and move their heads right round on their shoulders. When they need to turn their heads, they can do so nearly 360° until they mark a wood mouse in the litter. When they think the time is right they go off at that moment. Their feet make one little scratch but that doesn't matter because the mouse jumps and thinks: "Good God, it's too late".

This beautiful big soft-flying cat comes down and its

Barn Owl

zygodactyl (4 toe grip) feet reach for the prey's chest region – and that's it".

Talking about mice makes Jack think of a strange story to exemplify ecology at work.

"A wood mouse took the grub from a wild bee's nest and so affected the number of bees which were fertilising the clover. This affects the clover crop which in its turn affects the milk yield on any particular field. It's a long term thing but all these things have their effect. Now, village cats prey on mice so they'll affect the number of wood mice. The old story goes that unmarried ladies in the past always kept a cat and so this little bit of unintentional ecology was that the number of unmarried ladies in any particular area had an indirect effect on the milk yield. It's a crazy story but this is the complex way in which ecology does work".

Jack continues; "I was lying in the pink thrift on the Isle of Rathlin. Imagine it folks. Puffins whirring round me in circles. Above me a peregrine's nest with three chicks in the cliff-face. The female peregrine soared up, the male just behind her. She swooped down in a 300 ft. power dive, making a turn that would have ripped out the undercarriage of an aeroplane, and soared up again...wonderful!

On another occasion, I was watching a hawker dragonfly an aerial predator picking off the purple hairstreak butterflies that fluttered in the tops of oak trees. Then a young hobby swept down to seize the golden dragonfly. It bit off the wings letting the golden wings drop down to the ground. It was then that I realised the complexities of food chains. Food chains are much more complex than any of us imagine. Hairstreaks feeding on the aphid honeydew of oak leaves. Hawker dragonflies predating the butterflies. The hobby – a bird of prey – hunting down the dragonflies.

Up on the moorland, I have watched meadow pipits feeding on hairy caterpillars of the Emperor moth...another food chain...caterpillars feeding on the heather...meadow pipits feeding on the caterpillars...merlin feeding on meadow pipits...meadow pipits victimised by cuckoos.

I've watched a pair of meadow pipits struggling to satisfy a young tyke of a cuckoo twice their size. Always hungry, always begging for more, opening its orange gape for caterpillers...and the lovely bubbling trill of the female cuckoo

Duncraig Castle

in the distance.

I remember standing very still and quiet in a hedgerow as a female cuckoo sneaked into a dunnock's nest. The dunnock had slipped away for a moment and she'd seized her chance to lay her egg; she would seize her chance to lay eggs in the nest of other cuckolded dunnock foster parents".

Here comes another story, again in Scotland.

'Lochs and peaty islands in – one mile, an hour – walking country. I see a lovely little red-necked phalarope, light as a cork, like a floating bubble, paddling and spinning round to disturb the beetles and flies, and gnats, picking them daintily off the surface.

It's a beautiful sight, folks!"

Tan-y-Bwlch Field Centre, North Wales

Here we are in the beautiful Welsh countryside staying in an Adult Centre which overlooks a valley, a river and where we can see the little Ffestiniog Railway which is so popular with visitors.

Our group consists of the usual 15 or so enthusiasts prepared to walk and climb with Jack Otter.

"I am an ecologist" Jack says, "and if you want to know my definition, it is anyone at any level who is interested in the interplay of the communities of animals and plants that live around us and the fascinating way in which they inter-relate. We can't study any one thing in a vacuum".

"The wonderful basic miracle of life is photosynthesis. It is solar energy converted into stored energy in the form of carbohydrates".

The area in which we find ourselves is ecologically magnificent. There are mountains and woods leading down to sand dunes where we are likely to see marram grass which stabilises the dunes. Scabious, haresfoot, clover and eyebright. grow there.

The Linnet

One of the members says: "That plant is often eaten by short-sighted linnets!"

A great deal of discussion and amusing comments go on and Jack enjoys this as much as we all do.

We walk on the sandy beach and find lizards hurrying from

one clump of marram grass to another.

"Animals are creatures of habit just as we are. It is especially important as we grow older. Drill in the Army is important, it helps when you are under pressure. Makes life run smoother. It is a means of survival".

An argument then ensues with some of us but Jack sticks to his point of view. One of the group thinks that life would be boring if we did everything out of habit.

"No" says Jack, "mundane things should be done out of habit which then leaves time for the exciting things in life like natural history".

"Well folks, enthusiasm is everything. My wife says: most good men never grow up and I say, no, they don't but it's a grand life".

"When my son was little I taught him to love the natural world, because although I realised that the academic side of things is absolutely necessary, to get the real enthusiastic approach which gives people a lifelong love of these things, you've got to go a little further and learn the real joy of things. I taught him, to sit on the bank of a stream or a river where the big *ashnae* (dragonflies) were hunting. Then to make little bits of paper, wet them, and roll them into little balls like Beecham's pills. Have a small handful of them and when the *ashnae* come by, shoot them out with the thumb into mid-air".

Tan-y-Bwlch

Jack says: "Watch the *ashnae* home in on them fast like that, but never take them. Their eyesight is good and when they get within 8 or 10 inches of the paper balls they just ignore them. But if there was a fly there, they would take the fly. Flying two miles is nothing to this creature. These are the things we enjoy together, my son and I. He might not admit it but I think it was all these little things that gave him the great joy he has in the natural world".

While we are staying in Wales we are going to visit the Italian village of Port Meirion. Jack warns us:
"If you find you've got to go back for anything on our trips, bring it in the first place instead!"

The Grasshopper Warbler

On one of our walks we hear a most unusual bird song. It sounds like fishing tackle being pulled in. It is a grasshopper warbler. The Latin name is *locustella*.

"I've watched one singing, he comes up over a bramble spray singing with real ecstasy and his wings are out and his tail's out and you can see the sun shining through the webbing and his beak wide open and his throat extended and he's swaying from side to side to spin the song all over his territory and there's this wonderful reeling song. He's going one foot over the other up the bramble spray over the top and down again. It's an absolutely weird, thrilling experience".

East Bergholt, Suffolk

Flatford Mill Field Centre, Suffolk

We arrive in Constable country and see it the way it must have been when he was painting.

We recognized Willy Lott's cottage, we actually stayed there and Bill would comment on the low ceilings, holding his head,and that the people must have been quite short 150 years ago.

Willy Lott's Cottage – Photographed by Bill Kind

It looks more immaculate than it did when the 'Haywain' was painted.

East Bergholt, the village next to Flatford Mill, is the birthplace of John Constable. It has other distinctions and we find it fascinating to walk round the village and look at the church and the bells which actually stand on the ground outside the church.

We walked for many miles along the embankment of the river

Stour. The grebes and teal are busy preparing for nesting. We watch one pair of moorhens, the female sitting on the nest while she watches the male looking for grass and food for her. Jack makes much of this. Relating it to human male and female relationships.

Flatford Mill Field Centre – photogrpahed by Bill Kind

The Field Centre where we are staying is being run by a Warden and his wife who clearly think we are still school-children. He tells us some of the ground rules which amuse us. We nicknamed the Warden 'God' and it adds some amusement to our stay when he gives us his little 'pep talks', after all, we are all mature students and some even older than him.

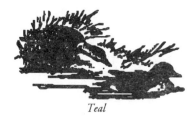

Teal

Knuston Hall, Northamptonshire

Knuston Hall is a country mansion. An elegant building of attractive proportions set in magnificent countryside in central Northamptonshire. Since 1951 adult education courses have been held here under the auspices of Northamptonshire County Council.

We are here for another of Jack's weekends in this pleasant and comfortable country house.

After Jack arrives, he prepares the evening's discussion by putting some headings on the blackboard in the lounge used for our tutorials.

This time he intends to talk about voles, stoats and weasels, mammals we are likely to come across on our walks.
But his intentions do not always materialise because he is easily side-tracked by a question!

Voles:

> 1. water voles.
> 2. short-tailed field voles.
> 3. long-tailed bank voles.

Field Vole Tracks

Knuston Hall

Jack says:

"The field vole is dependent on grass. Its whole life is grass. It lives in grass, runs in grass, it has its little highways in grass, builds its nest in grass, eats grass, and it makes love in grass. I'm quite sure if you could speak to a field vole, it would tell you that everything else you said was rubbish: the world's all grass.

It is the miracle of life: grass, photosynthesis, chlorophyll. The miracle of life. The chain of natural history is so complex, it sometimes frightens me.

Grass, photosynthesis, chlorophyll, they are just three in that chain. A chain can have a dozen links. It can have branches which come back and operate on themselves.

The leaf mosaic of the beech catches sunlight. Only plants make food, we process it. Leaves position themselves 'like people getting ready for a group photograph'.

There are beech trees in Charnwood Forest with bracken growing around them, nothing can grow in that circle because of excluded light".

Some of his older students know how he dislikes rhododendrons for the same reason.

"They only bloom for a short time, look good, take up a lot of space and nothing can grow underneath them. It's such a waste and what's more they were imported into this country. Ridiculous.

Knuston Hall

Stoats:

They are vicious savage killers, except badgers who are part of that family.

Stoat Tracks

If a male stoat was as big in size as a Bengal tiger it would have it for its dinner.

I once watched a stoat coming down the side of a hedge in typical Midlands country just like this and he had a beautiful speckled song thrush in his mouth. It was dead and down its lovely fawn speckled breast were big drops of arterial blood dropping on the ground. He was holding his head high because he's only got little legs so that he kept the thrush off the ground and he was trotting along at the side of the hedge with his beautiful red meat that he'd killed but before that, the thrush had been living on snails.

Snails:

Gastropods – one of the large groups of molluscs. Snails walk on their bellies in damp situations. They act as the meat for the thrush. Snails feed on various plants. There we are, back to photo-synthesis. There is your chain from stoat to plant. The soil depends on the parent rock, and so back to basics and the chain I was telling you about earlier".

From Knuston Hall we go on various excursions one of which is Monks Wood, a Nature Reserve for which Jack has to have a special permit. That in itself is a privilege, the result being that our group of around 15 students, do not meet anyone else during our visit.

Knuston Hall

Monks Wood
(Photographed by Anne Kind)

The wood belongs to the Nature Conservancy Council. It is a peaceful and beautiful place situated on the clay plateau at the southern edge of the Cambridgeshire Fenlands about 10 kilometres north west of Huntingdon, in the East Midland Region.

The reserve was purchased by the Nature Conservancy Council in two parcels: Monks Wood itself in 1953 and West Wood in 1954. The reserve was established to protect an example of the ash-oak woodland of the East Midlands. Much of the present day reserve is primary woodland. That is to say it has been woodland throughout recorded history. Rich and diverse ground flora includes bluebells, primroses and other attractive Spring flowers. There is a wild service tree, birds-nest orchids, crested cow wheat, small teasel – a remarkable range of butterflies can be found.

As we enter the wood, a path runs down on the left with trees meeting above and forming a tunnel, a vista with primroses running all the way as far as the eye can see. There is a feeling of magic here which I never experience anywhere else. Jack assures us that we shall hear nightingales, that is, if we listen and do not talk. He is right. A family of nightingales with their nest under close growing bushes on our left are being fed and the male is singing lustily.

Jack disillusions us by saying: "All he is doing is declaring his territory".

At this point he recalls his younger days and a slightly emotional note creeps into his voice. "I remember standing at the top of Tugby Wood about 30 years ago and listening to 7 cock nightingales on full song at the same time. It was a May night around 9 o'clock, the moon coming up over Loddington Woods. It was beautiful.

Nightingale

On another occasion early one morning I went into Loddington Wood and there was a pair of nightingales getting really hot about mating. The cock was singing to the hen like he does just before he actually mates. Anyone who has bred canaries will know this. However lovely a bird sings when it's what the bird fanciers call 'singing down for mating', it's different and it's better than you've ever heard just for a few minutes.

This nightingale was singing like this in a hawthorn bush and I sat in the next hawthorn bush, and the hen was in the hawthorn bush preening herself, you know how they do, and he was sitting on the top side of the bush and he was singing like this and he'd got the feathers under his throat out like this, wings and tail with the sun shining through and he was really letting it go. It was almost frightening because it was vibrant and I sat as near as that to him. Later on he would have a nest made of oak leaves at the bottom of the hazel stool. But he'd got to sing a bit more, she wasn't biting just then".

Whilst he talked, Jack used his hands to lend expression to his thoughts.

As we walked and found specimens to take back for the evening's lecture we found ourselves going deeper into this magical place until we came to a small lake, covered with duckweed and bulrushes.

I remember thinking of Shakespeare's Ophelia.

"Plants do things no animal would get away with" said Jack. "They exploit two or more areas, leaving one, going to another and coming back when the conditions are right. Duckweed floats on top and when the cold weather comes, some sink to the bottom into mud. When warm weather comes, chemical changes take place and healthy ones float to the surface again. Plants are wonderful".

Malham Tarn Field Centre, Yorkshire

The location of this fine building is a delight. On a sunny day the view takes in the Tarn, looking benevolent and beyond is Pen-y-ghent, 2227 ft. high. Beautiful on a fine day but when the weather changes, as it frequently does, the view becomes menacing. The Tarn is 1200 feet above sea level and has a slate bed beneath..This is one of the highest places in England where Great Crested Grebes breed.

Great Crested Grebes

We are told that this area has six different worlds or habitats: limestone, broadleafed woodland, tarn, (1500 ft. above sea level, limestone on a slate bed), watercourse, raised bog and heathland.

The soil is limestone. We see this for ourselves in great detail when we visit Malham Cove. It is a natural amphitheatre created by earth movements in the Ice Age.

It is the grikes we mainly remember on our visit to Malham Cove. They are at least 6 feet deep and form a limestone pavement. Walking across is an act of balance and is a memorable experience. We have to step carefully from clint to clint in order to cross the deep grikes, which because they are

51

sheltered from the elements contain plants of interest and distinction.

A short walk from the Cove we see Gordale Scar, a ravine at the head of which Gordale Beck plunges 300 feet in twin waterfalls.

A sparrowhawk flies at great speed, darts low into a field where it has obviously seen its prey. Jack tells us how they hunt down the side of hawthorn hedges at 40 miles per hour. Starlings can be feeding on the other side of the hedge and the hawk

Sparrowhawk

rolls over like a fighter aeroplane, goes straight in and picks up a starling from the flock.

We climb Pen-y-ghent and see the River Ribble below. There is a limestone cavern at Ling Ghyll on the Cam Beck, a tributary of the Ribble. Jack takes us to all these places and because he has no problems climbing or at least does not appear to have, he takes it for granted that we will be able to manage it too, although most of us are long past our prime.

That morning one of the group has found a fox earth. This gives Jack the opportunity during the evening lecture to talk about the fox and his predator – man – he has no other.

"If foxes got old and senile they would have a lingering death by starvation. He is like a dog but cat-like in grace and agility. He is a walker and a loner. Dogs nearly always trot in packs

Malham Tarn

but when you come across a fox he's nearly always walking and alone. His sense of hearing and sense of smell are good but his sight is poor.

I watched a fox once in Billesdon Coplow. He came within two yards of me and he never saw me. The wind was just in the right direction at that moment.

The fox has become an urban animal. In parts of London 20 fox earths in a 200 yard stretch have been counted. They feed alongside cats.

On the Continent the reservoir of rabies infection is the fox. We have 7 times as many foxes in this country. Once rabies is introduced into the fox community it will take off like a bomb. The problem will be with cats. A cat will kill a weak fox and bring rabies back into your home. I visited a rabies institute in India. It is a most horrible way of dying. I came away almost in a state of shock".

"The way a fox hunts" Jack continues, "is as follows:
Like a wolf following his prey a long way, trailing it. Once, in the snow, I found marks of a pheasant, then footprints of a fox following it. There were marks of wingtips blood and footprints with a long line at the side. Every three feet another spot of blood, 'It was all written in the snow'.

I saw two cock pheasants fighting. I peeped through hawthorn and watched. I saw a fox flat on the ground creeping forward like red smoke through the grass. Then he stopped and positioned himself like a cat, hindquarters moving, ready to spring, I couldn't bear any more and said: 'No, you don't....one pheasant went down the field, the other flew over the hedge.

I believe in fox hunting. It is by far a more humane and swift method of control than others.

Jack looks at us whilst he's talking:
"I learn a lot from my classes" he says. "And I tell you why, .. I pay attention!

There's a waterfall in the dales behind a wonderful arch and surrounded by rocks. As I stood there one day, a dipper flew straight through the cascading water with food in her beak. I knew she must have young. I'd got my wellingtons on and I waited until the mother flew out again and I waded across and put my arms into the waterfall....I could feel the nest and four tiny beaks.

Birds can't read but they're clever...they can't accept the edge of the nest being touched and bent. I've always been careful how I approach a nest.

Birds were my first love".

Painting Pictures with Words
Some of Jack's comments during our many walks

Plants are either a nuisance or well behaved.

The common spotted orchid is promiscuous.

Aspen, women's tongue, always moving. (Jack is careful not to go too far in sharing his opinions on female/male relationships, in case he is thought to be chauvinistic.)

In a heat wave all the dogs mercury faint.

Virginia creeper *(parthenocissus tricospidatum),* Jack can remember the Latin names for plants and animals. He did not receive secondary education.

Horsetail *(equiscutum)* was used as a pan-scraper.

Galls – the plant cells which are inspired to increase in size or in numbers or both by the presence of an invasive living organism. Both can live together without destroying each other – symbiotic.

Dogs – until there were 6 or 7 million dogs in this country (the vast majority un-trained), I loved dogs. Now?....Imagine the equivalent of 10 million people excreting in the streets...how would you like that?

Fir trees...Scots pine is not deformed...It grows like that. The Corsican grows straight, the Scots pine likes to mess about. Ash wood – it will burn when it's wet, it will burn when it's dry, fit for a queen to warm her slippers by.

Painting Pictures with Words

On Jean his wife....we have a symbiotic relationship...she needs me and I need her. She needs me to cook for, sew and do the decorating and the tax returns. It allows me to totally concentrate on what I love to do best...think about trees, birds and flowers and my Adult Education Courses.

At the age of 85 the most important things in my life: Jean...Trees...Single malt.

Leaves give me so much pleasure, beyond any understanding.

Rhododendrons are expensive to get rid of the bloody things. Nothing else grows where they grow. Once they have bloomed, that's that.

Nature conservation...5, 6, or 7 years cycle...sequence of coppicing, if done properly, is the finest way of conservation.

Bullfinch...its song is like a rusty hinge of a country gate after the piping has finished.

War...it was long periods of intense boredom mixed with short periods of intense fear.

I'm not a Yoga, I'm happy this way up.

Lesser celandine – just look at the gloss on those petals – as if they've been glossed over by someone from ICI!

Wild flowers? An old man said to me once, "It all depends on the soil, boy" – and it's true.

Painting Pictures with Words

Three dozen native trees in Britain. 1500 foreign trees. I'm not content with the three dozen. I want to know them all.

I can't take to twitching. The bush telegraph gets working like a tom-tom; and they travel all that way to look at a little brown shadow in a bush, tick it off, and travel all the way back again!

You can tell a ringed plover by its characteristic movements on the mud; it runs a little bit...stops...runs...stops: brrrrrr...click;
brrrrrr...click.

Lapwings begin to flock in June and July. But an old farmer used to say to me, "Going to get some bad weather, boy, plovers are moving".

Every Spring I'd stand in the wood to listen to the singing of the redstarts. "Oh my God, he's here again", they'd say.

Six robins sitting in the same bush on a Christmas card is an ornithological inexactitude.

Common chickweed – smooth, succulent; a good salad plant – better than your limp lettuce.

The laird interruped breakfast prayers to call his Maker's attention to the capercaille on the lawn, "God, – look at that caper!"

By the time I'm finished, the debt I owe will be immense.

On Jack Otter by one of his students:

*Three times the fun
Three talks in one.*

A list of venues for
Residential Courses organised by Jack Otter
between 1971 and 1993

1. The Convent, Hallaton, Leicestershire.
2. Launde Abbey, Leicestershire.
3. Knuston Hall, Northamptonshire.
4. Westham House, Barford, Warwickshire.
5. Flatford Mill, Suffolk.
6. Tan-y-Bwlch..Maentwrog, Gwynedd, North Wales.
7. Malham Tarn Field Centre, Yorkshire.
8. Adult Centre, Horncastle, Lincolnshire.
9. Burton Manor, The Wirral.
10. Highham Hall, Bassenthwaite, Lake District.
11. Clyne Halls of Residence, Gower.
12. University of East Anglia, Norwich.
13. Normal College, Bangor, Gwynedd.
14. Drapers Field Centre, Conway Valley.
15. Pollock Halls, University of Edinburgh.
16. Harlech College, Gwynedd.
17. Wolfson Hall, University of Glasgow.
18. Kindrogen Field Study Centre, Perthshire.
19. Duncraig Castle, Wester Ross.
20. Losehill Hall, Derbyshire.
21. The University of Kent at Canterbury.

In addition Jack ran many non-residential courses at various colleges in Northamptonshire and Leicestershire.

He broadcast on Radio Leicester from its inception for many years to which schoolchildren as well as adults listened and learnt.

Postscript

Jack Otter received an Honorary Degree of Master of Science from Leicester University in 1977, in recognition for the enormous amount of work he has done for Adult Education in the City and County.

He must have introduced thousands of people to the Natural World, people who may never have had their interest aroused before he came on the scene.

His enthusiasm is catching and when he calls you to look at a specimen, a flower, a plant or a bird we, his students, do as we are told and learn something.

Jack's words about the future: "I have lived a long time, I am now 85 years old. I've had a good life and I've had a lot of time to think.

I firmly believe that nuclear war will become irrelevent.

The Human Race will fade out on the ashes of a squandered paradise".

An Anthology

of

Verse

by

Anne Kind

inspired by thoughts

when on

Lecture Courses

led by

Jack Otter

Mrs. Anne Kind, OBE

By now you must be wondering about my connection with Jack Otter and why I should write his biography.

I am an uprooted plant. That's what Jack would call me. I was born in Berlin in 1922 and came to England in 1934. I was lucky, I managed to get out very early after the arrival of Hitler. My family, that is my parents and sister and all our furniture came too. But that's another story.

My husband, Robert William Kind, was born and bred in Leicestershire. There have been Kinds in this part of the country for about four hundred years. They came over to Britain with the Flemish weavers and after settling in Norfolk they moved inland and arrived in Leicestershire where they farmed and where some of their descendants still do, to this day.

Bill's father, Robert, was Headmaster of Long Street School, Wigston. In 1939 Bill – an only child – went to University College Hospital, London to study medicine. He qualified in 1942. He and I met during the war, while I was doing my nursing training and just before Bill was called up into the Army.

We married in 1943 and settled first in London where our two children were born and then moved to Leicestershire in 1949. Bill applied for, and got, the position of Medical Officer of Health for East Leicestershire and six years before his retirement, after re-organisation of the Health Service became Community Physician for North West Leicestershire. He retained his interest in Civil Defence and stayed as Scientific Officer for the County.

Anne Kind

He started the Family Planning Clinic in Leicester in 1954 in which I helped him. I then accepted the position of Branch Organiser, East Midlands, for the FPA with 14 clinics in my care.

In 1981 I started to work for LOROS, (Leicestershire Organisation for the Relief of Suffering), as Administrator and Fundraiser. My brief was to raise £1½ million with the specific aim to build a Hospice for the terminally ill in Leicester and Leicestershire. It was Bill's belief in me which made me accept the position and by 1985 the target had been reached and by the end of that year the first patients had been admitted. The Hospice is situated at the back of what was Groby Road Hospital, and was officially opened by the Prince and Princess of Wales in May 1986. I retired the following year.

Bill was always supportive and encouraged me in my work. We shared many interests such as archery, natural history, music and theatre.

Bill lectured on subjects in which he was knowledgeable and interested, particularly in the finer intricacies of archery. He was Coach to the Olympic Archery Team until his death in September 1987.

He was a good photographer and the thousands of slides which he took have been distributed among the RSPB and Jack's son Don. I have kept some. Reminders of our lifetime together.

Anne Kind

Jack and Bill shared a love of the countryside, both having been encouraged and had their curiosity aroused by their respective grandfather. They became good friends and when Bill died, Jack was devastated. "They don't make them like that anymore" he said, "he was a rare edition".

Bill taped many of Jack's lectures over the years. I remember asking him why he continued to make tapes of Jack's talks and he just smiled enigmatically. I expect he had it in mind to write up the story of Jack Otter.

When I asked Jack why someone shouldn't write up his story, his typical reply was "I thought you would never ask!"

In 1990 I received the OBE in the New Year's Honours List 'For services to the Community of Leicestershire'. An honour, for which I, as a foreigner, am very proud and it belongs in part to Bill.

Natural History

We are the flower people
Searching for specimens,
Exalting the brave
Who venture among rocks
Looking for alpines
Pansies, saxifrage.
Exotic names
Roll off our tongues
Like nursery rhymes.

Cameras click, notes compare,
Decrying daisies, extolling eyebright,

Bottoms up.

This was the first poem I wrote when we were walking with Jack.

I didn't know one plant from another and the botanists in our group were so enthusiastic, I felt quite isolated. So I wrote the poem and had a laugh in the last line – it's a typical view of botanists.

A Naturalist's Tale

I hear the song of the Nightingale
Amid the squelch of wellingtons.

The grass snake,
Patterned like a morse code print-out
Makes his slow and winding way.

Owl, the airborne cat
With talons for killing.
Silent feathers
Soft as cotton wool,
He uses his searchlight eyes
To make a living.

Cuckoo, all her kids in care
And up there the skylark
Its songpost, the wind.
A living dynamo singing
On top of his never-break voice.

London pride is burning
The birds are in full swing
Plants are nature's backcloth
Rocks and soil the base of everything.

The living world is always on the go
But don't forget that evolution's very slow.

Jack's Words

Over the years I heard Jack say all these words. All I have done is to
put them together and hope they ring bells for many of Jack's followers.

Orpheus

"When Orpheus sang, even the savage beasts came running to listen".

The tree was alive
With a thrush whose song
On a Winter's night
When the snow had gone
Was like a nightingale in Spring
On a churchyard tree
That bird was king.

And now I heard the bird again
A pitchblack night
In pouring rain
Its song descended
From the Jewry Wall*
Through Holy Bones
And gravestones
Came a magical call.

Since then his silence
Broke the spell
The hours go by
The tolling bell
Blackbirds and traffic noise are heard.
Orpheus has turned and fled
A magical bird.

* St. Nicholas Church, Leicester stands on the site of an ancient pagan temple.

Vaughan College is part of the site where the Jewry Wall is situated
in the centre of Leicester. The College has played a large part in
Jack's life as well as Bill's and mine.

This poem came 3rd in a poetry competition at East Leake.

All is not well in the countryside

The rook was dead,
Feet cut off,
Feathers spread like a fan,
Head on one side
Beak kissing the ground.

We stood around
Making assumptions.

Flies moved in
Making a meal.
Fox, rat and beetle
To come.

Ecology –
Recycling of bodies.

This was no natural death,
The rook had been shot.

Was it to be added
To someone's collection?

1987, Withcote near Launde

We had walked to Withcote from Launde when we saw the
dead rook. One of our group said, "Oh dear, he doesn't look
well!"

Launde in Autumn

We found dames violet and a daisy
Still in flower in November.
Lichen covered seat
Leaves crunching at our feet.
Their year ended.

Bright low Autumn sun
Cold wind, snow to come,
Every minute to be lived
And to remember
In December.

Autumn at Launde was always a refreshing experience. The house was very cold in Winter but at this time it was pleasant. I was sitting on the seat outside the beautiful old house and thought how it was good to be there although it would soon be Winter.

Jack likes the colder weather, he doesn't like Summer as many of us have heard him say.

I'm glad I wrote this little piece merely to remind myself of such a peaceful moment.

Charley

He walked slowly
In front of me
Superciliously
As if he knew

No one else in sight.
Would they believe me
When I tell them
Charley crossed my path today
His brush in full sway?

"It might have been a dog
Who can tell", they'd say.

"Aha, I'd reply, I can tell
By the foxy Charley smell".

I remember this occasion very well. Jack and the group had gone back to Launde Abbey for tea. Bill and I stayed on, he photographed a plant and I walked slowly ahead. The fox came from the right and walked across to the left of the path. 'Charley' is the nickname given to foxes by the hunting fraternity. But would the group believe me?

Spring At Launde

Chaffinch, breast like wine
Snowdrops in its wings
Beds of bugle
Blue as the sky
High in the ash tree
A blackbird sings.

Whitethroat, rising, falling flight
Paths grass covered flanked by pines,
Clouds have gathered, storm in sight
In the distance a church clock chimes.

The constant singing
Of warbler or wren
Marks the end of a splendid day
The wood is alive with campion
And the hawthorn is covered
With snowflakes in May.

Jack said "a chaffinch has 'snowdrops' in his wings".

All it means is that there is a white streak which contrasts beautifully with the "red breast like wine" (his words). He has such poetic ways of talking

In the last stanza, the hawthorn is covered with white blossom.

The Hunt

Laughton Hills

The fox stood in the hedgerow
On the hill like me
Transfixed
Watching, waiting.

The hunt moved down into the valley
Pinks on graceful thoroughbreds
Ever widening gap between them.

Red brush and I
When we'd recovered
From surprise at meeting
Couldn't help smiling.

Bill came home and told me that he had stopped the car and
watched the Fernie Hunt.

He had been there a few minutes when he realised he wasn't
alone. The fox had joined him and was watching too.

Late Autumn in Merrible Wood

Each year we visit Merrible
At every season.
Today it lies dark and misty
In the palm of a field.

Shots are heard.
Birds are disturbed.
An occasional leaf falls slowly,
Will lie fallow among thousands
To mulch away the Winter.

A ground spider's web
Covers the entrance
To the green lit world
Of the field vole.

A mole hole has been
Recently excavated.
Underground, in a dark tunnel
Must be a passing place for moles.
Someone has to give way.

On our last visit to Merrible this year
Clouds move fast, blue patches of sky appear
Somewhere in the distance, pigeons roost,
An owl hoots. A true November day.
It is time to put binoculars away.

Life Cycle

Painted lady
Gatekeeper, grayling
Meadow brown, admiral
Large white and small.

We walked on the railtrack
From Hadlow Road Station
Butterflies followed us
One and all.

Blue ones and pink ones
Admirals, ladies
Wall on red sandstone
Flew by our side...
We walked that old rail track from Hadlow Road Station
Where men from Hoylake
Built a railroad
And died.

Published, Co-Op Anthology, 1989

Thoughts on a walk while staying at Burton Manor, The Wirral, Cheshire. We walked with Jack over a disused railway track. The weather was perfect for butterflies; warm and sunny; hardly any wind.

Salcey Forest, 1986

If you want to survive
In the Forest of Salcey
You'll need a compass
Or it's sheer hell, see?

We lost our way
Walked round for hours
Forgot about bird song
And wild flowers.

We couldn't find
The wretched mark
We made with twigs
On bush or bark.

Jack was as puzzled
As you or I
Where was the sun
We'd lost the sky.

Just take my warning
You need to be fit
In Salcey
Or take a survival kit.

How can we forget getting lost in this vast forest in
Northamptonshire? To prevent it happening in the first place,
Jack had left sticks on branches of bushes and even then we
couldn't find our way back. I was having a laugh at this man
who knew so much about natural history but his sense of direction
was not so good.

Moments

I woke up early and I walked
Washing my feet in dew
Through lines of larch trees and Scots pines
I see a woman paint the view.

Above my head a wren
Is bursting with his song
The smallest bird and yet
He sings so loud and strong.

I walk through thick, lush grass
My feet are wet with dew
The bird has stopped his song
Nobody paints the view.

July 1987, Knuston

We have to get up early when we take part in Jack's courses.
I'm not too good early in the morning. However, on this occasion I walked through the grass around Knuston Hall and
explored the area around the animal cemetery. Someone else
was also up early.

I have many such lovely moments which I experienced on
our weeks or weekends with our friend.

Knuston Animal Cemetery

Recky, Trixy.
Trap and Tuiwi
Bucher, Simon
Ponto, pronto
Obedient servant
Of your master.
He is sleeping
While you're keeping
Watchful eyes
On sleeping master.
Next to you lies clever Florrie
Dear and kind
So gracious pussy
Trapped and killed
One rainy Sunday
By the London Midland Scottish.

Behind the trees at the back of the garden at Knuston Hall is an animal cemetery. There are headstones to cats and dogs going back nearly 100 years. At the end of the field adjoining the Hall is the main railway line which was once the L.M.S. Poor Florrie was killed by one of the trains.

I thought the cemetery a charming English eccentricity and the names were exotic except for Florrie, the cat.

Monks Wood

Trees meet
To form a lined vista.
Everywhere we look
Ragged robin
Buttercups, clover underfoot.

Cuckoo calls.
Thunder threatens.
We disturb a nest
Of nightingales.

Birch trees, orchids,
Constant bird song
Wren, garden warbler,
Black cap, nightingales.

This wood is full of magic.
Among the trees
We find a lake
Where Ophelia could have drowned.

This magical wood in the border country between
Cambridgeshire and Northamptonshire was such a surprise. We
were lucky enough to get permission to visit. Jack applied and
got it from the Nature Conservancy Council.

What a joy it is to picture it there and then, both with the
camera and with the pen.

It is my favourite wood. Anyway, we heard nightingales
here!

Sandy Nature Reserve...October 1986

A guelder rose lights up
This yellow Autumn day.
Fungi found and picked up...
Miniature flying saucers.

A single spangle gall
Detached from a leaf
Hangs on a cobweb
By a single gossamer thread.
Cobwebs have their uses.

Snatches of goldcrest and coal tit are heard,
While we pick and eat blackberries
Left to us by law-abiders.
Mouths, fingers, tongues, blood-red.

Varied experts, apart from Jack
Are giving lectures on botany
To new members or those who will listen.
Photographers wander off, writers write.
Jack's group follows its normal pattern.

This was a sunny day in Autumn and towards the end of the day group members began to wander off.

There is always something to see and write about. Simple things like picking blackberries make me remember this day.

Lincolnshire

Dolls houses
Farms and churches
On the vast horizon.

Roads coil round fields
Of dazzling yellow,
Pea green, potato brown, and
Clipped, unlayered hedges.
A patchwork quilt
Covered by blue sky.

Meadow pipits appear
From nowhere
Like paper darts, falling.

On salt marshes
Noisy skylarks rise
Diverting us from their nests,
Whilst the tide creeps in
Like a thief, beckoning us
To disrespect the moon.

Again, some of the lines in this poem are Jack's words. Jack
was warning us that the tide "creeps in like a thief" and that the
area where we are walking is dangerous.

Veronica

Lincolnshire

You are beautiful, veronica
In that small woodland patch
In the shade.
Farewell
Speedwell.

This small poem to a small blue plant was all I could say
about a corner behind the beach in Saltfleetby, Lincolnshire.

The phototographers among us would stop and so did I, to
recall my thoughts at that moment.

I only started to write to use my notes as a diary. It has stood
me in good stead, since.

Kirkby Wood

A stream moves slowly
In Kirkby Wood.
Edged by marigolds and king cups
And in the field beyond
Cows lie down to forecast rain.

River Bain flows to the Wash
Gold crest sings
Like a cork on a wet window.
Regulus, regulus, you're a little king.

Already we're at the end of May.
Bark drops from Scots pine
Leaving golden remains
Like a lioness' hide.

We were staying at Horncastle Adult Education Centre.

We walked over Kirkby Moors, Lincolnshire and through the woods on many occasions. It was here one Summer's day, after we had walked through the rain when the sun came out and made everywhere steam.

Suddenly we saw an adder, then another and another – they too had come out to sun themselves after rain. Altogether we counted 19!

Jack was in his element – he loves snakes.

Impressions of Suffolk

On our way to Constable's mill
We speed right up to the edge of the map
Pass rose covered thatched cottages
Pink or mustard yellow, edged with white.

The speedometer comes right down
To keep pace with a two wheeled buggy
Pulled by a horse, agile as a ballet dancer;
Reins held by a young descendent of Viking invaders.

Posters at every village proclaim galas galore;
Splashes of red are seen among golden uncut corn,
Grass verges on fire with bright poppies.

On our arrival, Willie Lott's cottage greets us,
Noisy ducks float by on the pond to complete the canvass.

I wrote this in the car going to Flatford. The scenery was
different from any I had seen before. It was the colours which
were so vivid, which intrigued me.

On a Suffolk Beach

Nash must have painted here
Decades ago, artist of war.
Shot down aircraft
Arranged themselves,
Modelled for him.

Black wooden sea defences
Became the background
For a painter's pallette.

Now shallow waves lap over them,
Tangled seaweed grows
On crosses, commemorating death.

The sea has lost the past
On silent Suffolk beaches.
Sand martins hide and seek
In crumbling cliffs;

The land is dying
While skylarks' song and sun
Beat down tenaciously.

I recognised the coastline from seeing Paul Nash's paintings.
This is a typical view while walking on the beach. The sea on
one side and the crumbling cliffs on the other. There are always
skylarks singing.

Remember Flatford

Warm fox droppings
Blackcap singing overhead
Walking boots are plodding
Red potato beds

Jack is marching on ahead
Doreen's bringing up the rear
Most of us are in between
Ernest's nowhere to be seen
He's lost again, I fear

Lorna with her drawings
Leslie with his galls
Doves continuous calling
Broad beans for dinner...meat balls

Lorna with her drawings
Leslie with his galls
Doves continuous calling
Broad beans for dinner...meat balls

Up the river, moorhens
Building up their nest
The male is doing all the work
The female is at rest

God is in his heaven
Grace is being said
Switch the lights out children
Before you go to bed

Lorna with her drawings
Leslie with his galls
Doves continuous calling
Broad beans for dinner...meat balls

Lorna with her drawings
Leslie with his galls
Doves continuous calling
Broad beans for dinner. .meat balls.

This was a wonderful week spent at the Flatford Mill Field Centre in Suffolk.

We picked up samples during the day and took them back to discuss in the evening.

One of our members was good at drawing – another an expert on galls; and from morning until midnight the doves were calling from the trees surrounding the Field Centre.

The food wasn't very good and one evening we had meat balls, and broad beans cooked in their pods! The warden treated us like schoolchildren and told us when to turn off the lights.

So we nicknamed him – 'God'.

Feed Time

We sit on the steps
Overlooking the Tarn.

Grassy slopes
Strewn with latin flowers.

Water as still,
As if it were frozen.

Not a breeze or ripple
On the lonely Tarn.

Insects buzz
Birdwatchers chew

Sudden movement
Raises binoculars

Spotted flycatcher
Beak full of insects.

"Swop you
For my meat paste sandwich".

Malham Tarn, Yorkshire

The food was not too good at this Field Centre and our sandwiches were very uninteresting. However, the view across the Tarn was glorious, and so was the bird life.

Ecology

I saw a grayling butterfly
Among the empty cans
But long ago
Before they sprayed, I saw
Hundreds of meadow brown
Like water shimmering
You never see that now.

I dropped a peach stone
On the Dales
Near rocks
On which we sat.

Soft luscious fruit
Hard stone
May grow
On Yorkshire soil.

If sprays allow
A hundred years from now
Maybe
There'll be a tree.

Published: *Dalesman* 1977

This was written when we stayed at the Malham Tarn Field Centre in Yorkshire. We had stopped for lunch and I dropped a peach stone, left it there and felt a bit guilty but consoled myself that one day there might be a tree.

The first stanza are Jack's words given during a talk.

The Tarn

Trees fight the gale today,
Water runs over resisting stones.
The ill-tempered Tarn
Spits windblown spray.

The sun brings peace.
Fishermen throw their lines
Sheep bleat, curlew call.
Can the Tarn be trusted?

It can become wild again.
Black, black water
Like shadows under eyes
To reflect an angry sky.

Malham Tarn, 1986

In The Beginning

The river rumbles and roars
Like a lion
Emerging from its cage

Winds and imprints itself
Into the side of the mountain.

Grey, green and blue rings,
Hollowed stone
Millions of years of erosion.
Deep set eyes
Filled with tears.

Wales 1978

Tan-y-Bwlch...1983

Little trains move slowly
Through the mountains.
I sit on Tan-y-Blwch Station
Listen to birds, goldfinch,
Nightingales, they sing on bushes
Rubbish heaps or anything.

"Salvation is the Lord" says the sign.
Where are the people who use this line?
Do they sit on the seats provided?
Or are they merely here for show
There are flowers by the railtrack
Do they watch the flowers grow?
English signs say 'teas and toilets'
Life in Wales is calm and slow.

Flowers in barrels
Waste bins provided
Old gas lamps revived
To light up the dark
Someone lives in the signal box.
.In the distance
A dog's faint bark.

Everyone loves this little Welsh station
There tomatoes are growing in the sun
Goldcrest and a wren are singing
On an empty platform, except for one.

This out of the way railway station is well known among visitors to
Wales. I sat on the platform and took notes of what I saw and heard in
this deserted place. It is part of the route taken by the Ffestiniog
Railway in the Snowdonia National Park.

We are staying at the Adult Centre. It was a hot Summer and walking
with our pack and binoculars was not always easy.

Harlech

It wouldn't be a woodsedge would it?
Sedges are wedges with edges, you see.
Jack Otter's small group are looking and finding
Interesting specimens by the sea.

Kath, two Pams, Marion and Alan
Gordon, Anne and Bill and Jack
Walk and stop and stop and walk
Carry on talking, carrying their pack.

Stonechat lands on the dunes at Harlech
Grasshoppers sing and the stones are heard
High above their throats are clicking
Stonechat, delightful little bird.

Common blues on the sea holly
Pipits' alarm as they rise and rise
People naked on the snowy white sand dunes,
And when we walked past them
They did look surprised.

This was a hot day during our stay at Tan-y-Bwlch Field
Centre, Wales.

We walked for hours and carried our lunch with us, dressed
for climbing. Made a detour and found the beach at Harlech
where we saw common blue butterflies. Pipits and stonechats
were heard and seen. What a shock to see nude bathers – we
envied them.

Delights of Summer

We walked the valley for six hours
Looking for birdlife and wild flowers
Long hot days not far away
Heady scent of flowering may
But the cuckoo calling twice a minute
Makes me wish he twitters like a linnet.

Pennant Valley, Wales

I long to hear the cuckoo each Spring but on this occasion, I'd had
more than enough of his voice!

Life

Black, black, black
Is the forest of pines.
Nothing grows
No life among the needles.
Perched high
On the topmost branch
Of a conifer,
A secret bird sings,
Not to be seen.

Scotland 1978

We had been walking through a forest near Plockton, Wester Ross in Scotland.

It was very peaceful and the only sound I heard was from a single bird. It was invisible, I tried to look for it with my binoculars but could not find it. I was unable to distinguish between different bird songs at that time.

Jack has taught us a lot since our early days of bird-watching.

On The Isle Of Skye

Muriel on Skye
Found a flower
Bright yellow
In a crevice of rock
Caused by laval intrusion,
Leant forward to reach it
Slipped over and fell
Bridging millions of years
In the split of a second.

We had a beautiful week's holiday in Scotland with Jack,

We took the ferry to Skye and were amazed by the wild flowers we saw and by the natural beauty of the place.

Where is the Sun?

It's raining and it's blowing gales
In Scotland, England and in Wales.
Ernest's got new walking boots
He's got to get some wear from them
Can't wear them with his suits
So bring the sunshine back, Jack
Please can we have some sun
Where's your hotline to above?
Ask heaven what we've done
To deserve rain, mud and gales, Jack
Even snow and hail...no sun.
Can't botanize whilst raining, Jack
So bring us back some sun.

One day during our stay in Suffolk, we had appaling weather.
   This poem of pleading was heartfelt on behalf of our group.
   It is well known that during Jack's courses the weather would
be fine. This was an exception. Bill called it "Jack's hotline to
heaven" – it had snapped that day!

Bells of East Bergholt

The bells of East Bergholt
Are ringing and singing
The children are bringing
Their pennies and silver
To encourage the ringers
To ring bells at East Bergholt.

In the graveyard they ring them
Where the bells are now found
When the church tower was built
They ran out of money
So the bells were left on holy ground.

The ringers are strong ones
Some short ones, some tall ones
It really is an unusual sight
They swing them and sing them
On this wooden platform
They swing those bells
With all of their might.

Bell of East Bergholt
On Sundays you ring
For hours on end
From morning to night.

This evokes the memory of our stay at Flatford when some of us
went to the next village on the Sunday after our arrival.

It was a very memorable occasion.

(see page 42)

Ode to Jack Otter

Jack, Jack
Come and see this
Come and see that
I've just seen a lovely bird.
Jack, Jack, listen to that song
Was that the nightingale we heard?

Pendulous sedges
Orchids that's spotted
Orange tip, cuckoo spit
Ivy that's knotted
Duckweed, comfrey
Robin that's ragged
Jack, there's a bird
With a long tail, it wagged.

Jack, Jack, which way to go back?
We want to know at the end of the day
This way? No, that way.
Jack shakes his head and says "nay"
"That's not the way we came folks
Over there's the way we came
If you want to get back
Collect up your pack
And make for the opposite way".

Jack, Jack
There's a print in the sand
Is it a big bird, a small bird, a black bird
Or is it a bird in the hand ?

Jack looks and peers
Then whistles
He smiles as he quietly hissed
"It's lame and pied
And I think it's one eyed
And it's not on the British list".   *Knuston 1983*

I think this poem says it all. Fifteen people kept calling Jack to look at various specimens. When it came to the time to get back to Knuston Hall (in time for Jack to have his pint before dinner), he frequently couldn't remember the way back. So I had a little dig at his lapse of memory.

The last stanza is Jack teasing us. He often talked of plants or birds either being on the British list or not, whichever the case may be.

Birds fly away so quickly, it is easy for us to mistake what we have seen. We can only try to describe it to Jack – his response is his little joke.

Retirement

*A farewell presentation, held in March 1994, at Vaughan College
to mark Jack's retirement after 35 years as a natural history tutor in the
Department of Adult Education at Leicester University*

(photograph Leicester Mercury)

Retirement

Jack and Jean Otter listening to Anne Kind

Well...I have to say something!

Jack with his son Don, together with Bill Kind

Books by Jack Otter

The Birds of East Leicestershire
illustrated by John Stacey
Loughborough Naturalists' Club, 1965, pp. 80
(out of print)

and

The Birds of Bradgate
illustrated by John Stacey
The Bradgate Park Trust, 1974, pp. 45

Other titles by Anne Kind

Poetry publications

View in a Rear Mirror
1982, £1.00

and

Selective Memories
1989, £1.50

Both published by Anne Kind

all proceeds to

L O R O S
HOSPICE CARE FOR LEICESTERSHIRE

To Order
Please contact Volcano Publishing

Other titles from Volcano

Title	Author	Published	Price
Pawnshops and Lard	*Jack Francis*	1989	£3.55
Polly and Alice	*Winifred Ruston*	1990	£4.70
A Wife on the Walk	*Elizabeth Gregson*	1992	£3.55
Rural Medical Practice	*R. Graham Lilly*	1993	£3.85
Lutterworth Police Station	*Ann Amos*	1993	£1.35
A Wife on the Alt. Pennine Way	*Elizabeth Gregson*	1993	£3.55
Lutterworth Past & Present	Volcano	1994	£1.60

Please send s.a.e.
for full details and order form for any of the above.

Please allow 14 days for delivery.

All prices include post and packing

New for 1995

BRADGATE

by

David Ramsey

A well researched history of Bradgate, the park and surrounding villages. David Ramsey provides not only a chronological history but also the affect on those who lived and worked on the estate. He lists occupations, where and when they lived, and even the animals kept by them.

Originally planned for publication in 1994 but held back due to the size of the manuscript and that further information on roof timber dating of the cottages was being carried out by Loughborough University using the new ring-dating method. This has now be added to the manuscript.

Bradgate will almost certainly be of more than one volume as some parts will be of more general interest than others.

Please contact Volcano if you would like to have advance details of the books under this title.

V·O·L·C·A·N·O
PUBLISHING